A New True Book

PRESIDENTS

By Carol Greene

CHILDREN'S PRESS
A Division of Grolier Publishing
Sherman Turnpike
Danbury, Connecticut 06816

Fireworks display marked the inauguration of Ronald Reagan as president of the United States.

PHOTO CREDITS

Black Star—©Dennis Brack, 10, 19 (left), 21 (left), 22 (bottom); ©Owen D.B., 13

Historical Picture Services, Inc.—8 (left)

Hillstrom Stock Photo—21 (right)

John F. Kennedy Library—19 (right), 20, 22 (top)

Nawrocki Stock Photo—©Jim Whitmer, 24

Roloc Pictorial Research—2, 8 (right), 9, 45

Stock, Boston, Inc.—©Stacy Pick, 12

Uniphoto Picture Agency—4, 6 (2 pictures); ©Michael J. Pettypool, 13 (left); ©Michael Evans, 13 (right); ©Paul Conklin, 15; ©Mark Reinstein, 17 (left); Official White House Photo—©Bill Fitz-Patrick, 17 (right)

AP/Wide World Photos—43 (bottom right)

Department of Treasury, Bureau of Engraving and Printing—25-43

©Reinhard Brucker—cover

Cover: Mount Rushmore

This book is for Carolyn Canavan and Erica Schweizer

Library of Congress Cataloging in Publication Data

Greene, Carol.
    Presidents.

    (A New true book)
    Includes index.
    Summary: Explains what the job of the president is and briefly introduces the first forty presidents of the United States, from George Washington through Ronald Reagan.
    1. Presidents—United States—Juvenile literature. 2. United States—Politics and government—Juvenile literature. [1. Presidents. 2. United States—Politics and government] I. Title. II. Title: Presidents of the United States.
EI76.8.G74   1984   973′.09′92 [B]   84-7719
ISBN 0-516-01928-7   AACR2

TABLE OF CONTENTS

Prime Minister Winston Churchill of Great Britain (left), President Franklin D. Roosevelt of the United States (center), and Russia's Joseph Stalin, leader of the Union of Soviet Socialist Republics (right), met to discuss political and military subjects during World War II.

THE PRESIDENT'S JOB

The president of the United States has an important job. It is one of the most important jobs in the world.

Presidents are elected for four years. This is called a term. Until 1951, presidents could be elected again and again. Franklin D. Roosevelt served three terms and part of a fourth.

Political parties (above) meet to vote for the individual they want to run for the office of president of the United States. People (below), over the age of eighteen who have registered to vote, can vote for a new president every four years.

But in 1951, the U. S. Constitution was amended, or changed. Now a president may serve no more than two terms—or eight years.

Presidents are elected every four years on the first Tuesday after the first Monday in November. People from all fifty states in the United States vote.

Then, on January 20 of the next year, the winner

George Washington (left) was the first
president to take the oath of office.
One hundred eighty-eight years
later Jimmy Carter (above) took the same oath.

is inaugurated, or officially
takes the office of
president.

This is what presidents
promise to do:

"I do solemnly swear
that I will faithfully execute

Presidents take the oath of office in a public ceremony held on the steps of the Capitol.

the office of president of the United States, and will to the best of my ability, preserve, protect and defend the Constitution of the United States."

President Gerald Ford, as head of the executive branch of government, signs a tax law sent to him by Congress.

Presidents must see that all laws of the United States government, called federal laws, are carried out. They must keep the country peaceful.

Presidents are in charge of one part of the government—the executive branch. There are two other parts in our government—the legislative branch and the judicial branch. They each have special jobs.

Congress is made up of the House of Representatives and the Senate.
Congress is the legislative, or lawmaking, part of the government.

The legislative branch is
Congress. It includes the
House of Representatives
and the Senate. They pass
the laws.

The Supreme Court (left) is the judicial branch of the government. Chief Justice Warren Burger (above left) gives the oath of office to Sandra Day O'Connor. Justice O'Connor is the first woman to serve on the highest court in the United States.

The Supreme Court and its lesser federal courts are the judicial branch of government. The court decides if a law is right or wrong. According to the

U. S. Constitution, this court protects all the people in America from unjust laws.

The president must work with the lawmakers in Congress and the justices of the court.

More than three million people work for the United States government. Presidents must see that the work they do runs smoothly. They do this by

President Ronald Reagan meets with his cabinet regularly.

picking people to be in
charge of different parts of
the government.

Presidents pick people to
serve on the cabinet. Each
cabinet member is in
charge of one department.

The thirteen cabinet offices are:

- secretary of state
- secretary of the treasury
- secretary of defense
- attorney general
- secretary of the interior
- secretary of agriculture
- secretary of commerce
- secretary of labor
- secretary of health and human services
- secretary of housing and urban development
- secretary of transportation
- secretary of energy
- secretary of education

Presidents pick the best people to head each department.

Presidents also pick ambassadors to represent

President Reagan picked Jeane Kirkpatrick (left) to be ambassador to the United Nations and Donald Rumsfeld (right) to be his special ambassador to the Middle East.

the United States in other countries.

The Senate must approve the presidents' choices for ambassadors, cabinet offices, and Supreme Court justices.

President Anwar el-Sadat of Egypt (left), President Jimmy Carter of the United States (center), and Prime Minister Menachem Begin of Israel (right) sign a treaty, or agreement.

Presidents work with other countries. They make agreements with heads of other countries. They meet with them to talk about problems.

President Carter (left) greeted Prince Faud of Saudi Arabia (left),
and President Kennedy (right) awarded a medal at a special ceremony.

Sometimes presidents
give medals to people who
have done something
special. They give parties
for important visitors from
other countries.

President Kennedy, as commander in chief of the armed forces, inspected an armored tank unit at Fort Stewart, Georgia.

Presidents are also leaders of the two million people in the armed forces. They must be sure the armed forces are run correctly. The president is the only person who can give permission to use nuclear weapons.

Presidents Ford (left), a Republican, and Carter (right), a Democrat, rode in parades and gave speeches throughout the United States to help their political parties win elections.

Presidents work for their political parties, too. A president may help a person win a political office in his or her state.

Presidents Kennedy (above) and Carter (below) met with
working people and listened to their problems.

Finally, presidents must work for all the people of the United States. They must talk with the people and tell them what is happening. They must show people that they are good leaders.

Today presidents get paid $200,000 a year. They also get extra money for travel and other special

The White House is the president's home.

things. They live with their families in the White House in Washington, D.C.

After they leave the office of the president, they continue to be paid money as long as they live. This money is called a pension.

THE PRESIDENTS OF THE UNITED STATES

1. George Washington (1732-1799)

George Washington grew up in Virginia. He became head of the American army during the revolutionary war. In 1789 he became the first president of the United States and served until 1797.

GEORGE WASHINGTON

2. John Adams (1735-1826)

John Adams worked in politics for many years. He served as president from 1797 to 1801. During that time many people argued about how our new nation should be governed. He was the first president to live in the White House.

JOHN ADAMS

THOMAS JEFFERSON

3. **Thomas Jefferson** (1743-1826)
Thomas Jefferson studied science, music, education, art, and more. He wrote the Declaration of Independence and worked for religious freedom. He was president from 1801 to 1809. He was the first president inaugurated in Washington, D. C.

4. **James Madison** (1751-1836)
James Madison worked hard for the U. S. Constitution. He was president from 1809 to 1817. During that time the U. S. fought the War of 1812 with England.

5. **James Monroe** (1758-1831)

James Monroe was president from 1817 to 1825. He said that countries in Europe must not take any more land in North or South America. This is called the Monroe Doctrine.

JAMES MONROE

6. **John Quincy Adams** (1767-1848)

John Quincy Adams was the son of President John Adams. He served as president from 1825 to 1829. He worked for freedom and conservation.

ANDREW JACKSON

7. **Andrew Jackson** (1767-1845)
Andrew Jackson was the son of a poor farmer. He grew up to be a fine soldier. Many people admired him and he was president from 1829 to 1837. He was the first president to be nominated by a political party at a national convention.

8. **Martin Van Buren** (1782-1862)
Martin Van Buren's father owned a tavern. Martin grew up to be a lawyer and a clever politician. He was president from 1837 to 1841.

9. William Henry Harrison (1773-1841)

William Henry Harrison was a soldier and a farmer. He loved the West and lived in Ohio. He became president in 1841, but died one month later.

10. John Tyler (1790-1862)

Vice-president John Tyler became president when William Henry Harrison died in 1841. He did not get along with Congress. He served only until 1845. He was the father of fifteen children.

JAMES K.POLK

11. **James K. Polk** (1795-1849)

James K. Polk was president from 1845 to 1849. He fought a war with Mexico for land in the Southwest. He also tried to get more land in the Northwest.

ZACHARY TAYLOR.

12. **Zachary Taylor** (1784-1850)

Zachary Taylor was a famous soldier. He became president in 1849. But he died in 1850 before he could do much as president.

MILLARD FILLMORE

13. **Millard Fillmore** (1800-1874)

Vice-president Millard Fillmore became president in 1850 when Zachary Taylor died. He did not like slavery, but he did not work hard against it. So the North voted against him and he had to leave office in 1853.

14. **Franklin Pierce** (1804-1869)
Franklin Pierce was a handsome
soldier and a clever politician. He
served as president from 1853 to
1857. He was for slavery and
made many enemies.

15. **James Buchanan** (1791-1868)
James Buchanan was for slavery,
too. He served as president from
1857 to 1861. During that time the
states came closer and closer to
fighting each other over slavery.

JAMES BUCHANAN

16. Abraham Lincoln (1809-1865)
Abraham Lincoln was president from 1861 until he was shot and killed in 1865. "Honest Abe" hated slavery and said that all slaves in the U. S. were to be free. He led the U. S. through the Civil War.

ANDREW JOHNSON

17. Andrew Johnson (1808-1875)
Vice-president Andrew Johnson became president in 1865 when Abraham Lincoln was killed. He wanted public schools and more land for farmers. But he made many enemies in Congress and he was nearly impeached. Only one vote saved him from being removed from office. He left office in 1869.

18. Ulysses S. Grant (1822-1885)
Ulysses S. Grant was a popular general in the Civil War. He served as president from 1869 to 1877. During that time the country worked hard to make the South strong again.

ULYSSES S. GRANT.

19. Rutherford B. Hayes (1822-1893)
Rutherford B. Hayes was a soldier and a lawyer. He served as president from 1877 to 1881. But there was a lot of arguing with Congress and he couldn't do much.

RUTHERFORD B. HAYES

JAMES A. GARFIELD

20. James A. Garfield (1831-1881)

James A. Garfield was a poor boy who grew up to be a teacher, a soldier, and a politician. He became president in 1881. But six months later he died after being shot.

CHESTER A. ARTHUR

21. Chester A. Arthur (1829-1886)

Vice-president Chester A. Arthur became president when James A. Garfield was killed in 1881. He worked hard to make the government more honest. Arthur served as president until 1885.

22 and 24. **Grover Cleveland**
(1837-1908)
Grover Cleveland was president twice—from 1885 to 1889 and from 1893 to 1897. He was an honest man and tried to keep the government honest. But the country had many business problems during his second term.

GROVER CLEVELAND

23. **Benjamin Harrison**
(1833-1901)
Benjamin Harrison served as president from 1889 to 1893. He was grandson of the ninth president, William Henry Harrison. Benjamin tried to make businesses in the U. S. more successful.

BENJAMIN HARRISON

35

WILLIAM M°KINLEY

25. **William McKinley** (1843-1901)

William McKinley became president in 1897. He helped big businesses at home and made the U. S. more powerful in other parts of the world. He had just begun to serve a second term in 1901 when he was killed.

THEODORE ROOSEVELT

26. **Theodore Roosevelt** (1858-1919)

Vice-president Theodore Roosevelt became president in 1901 when William McKinley was killed. He believed in conservation and had the Panama Canal built. Many people loved "Teddy" and he served until 1909. He was the first president to visit another country while in office.

27. William Howard Taft
(1857-1930)

William Howard Taft was president from 1909 to 1913. He loved peace, but he had many problems in his government. Taft tried to help big businesses. Taft was six feet tall and weighed three hundred pounds. He was the largest president.

WILLIAM HOWARD TAFT

28. **Woodrow Wilson** (1856-1924)

Woodrow Wilson was president from 1913 to 1921. During this time the U. S. fought in World War I. Wilson helped small businesses and working people. Wilson was unsuccessful in getting the U. S. to join a world family, the League of Nations. He was the first president to have regular meetings with the press and to speak on the radio.

WOODROW WILSON

WARREN G. HARDING

29. **Warren G. Harding**
(1865-1923)
Warren G. Harding was president from 1921 until he died in 1923. He helped big businesses and kept the U. S. Navy from growing too fast. Some dishonest men in his government caused many problems.

CALVIN COOLIDGE

30. **Calvin Coolidge** (1872-1933)
Vice-president Calvin Coolidge became president in 1923 when Warren Harding died. He made the government more honest and the country richer. He served until 1929.

31. Herbert C. Hoover
(1874-1964)

Herbert C. Hoover was president from 1929 to 1933. During that time many businesses in the U. S. went broke. Hoover tried to get jobs for people, but many felt he did not help enough.

HERBERT HOOVER

32. Franklin D. Roosevelt
(1882-1945)

Franklin D. Roosevelt did much to help people without jobs. He led the country through most of World War II. He was president from 1933 until he died in 1945. He was president for over twelve years. He was the first president to speak on television.

FRANKLIN D. ROOSEVELT

33. Harry S. Truman (1884-1972)

Vice-president Harry S. Truman became president in 1945 when Franklin Roosevelt died. He helped countries that had suffered in World War II. Later he sent U. S. soldiers to fight in Korea. He was president until 1953.

34. Dwight D. Eisenhower (1890-1969)

Dwight D. Eisenhower was a popular general during World War II. "Ike" became president in 1953 and served until 1961. He ended the fighting in Korea.

35. **John F. Kennedy** (1917-1963)
John F. Kennedy came from a family that loved politics. He became president in 1961 and worked hard for equal rights for all people. He also worked for the arts. In 1963 he was shot and killed.

36. **Lyndon B. Johnson** (1908-1973)
Vice-president Lyndon B. Johnson became president in 1963 when John Kennedy was killed. He served until 1969. War in Vietnam made Johnson's time as president a hard one.

RICHARD NIXON

GERALD R FORD

JIMMY CARTER

37. **Richard M. Nixon** (1913-   )
Richard Nixon became president in 1969. He got along well with many foreign countries. Because of scandal, Nixon had to resign in 1974. He was the first president to resign from office.

38. **Gerald R. Ford** (1913-   )
Vice-president Gerald Ford became president in 1974. He tried to help people regain their trust in government. Ford served until 1977. He is the only person to serve as vice-president and president that was not elected.

39. **Jimmy (James Earl) Carter** (1924-   )
Jimmy Carter was president from 1977 through 1981. He had problems with Russia and Iran. But he led peace talks between Israel and Egypt.

40. Ronald Reagan (1911-   )

Ronald Reagan became president in 1981. The U. S. had problems with money then. Reagan tried to help businesses by leaving them alone. He served until 1989.

41. George Bush (1924-   )

George Bush served as Ronald Reagan's vice-president. He became president himself in 1989. President Bush solved a number of international problems. But job growth in America slowed during his term. He served until 1993.

42. Bill (William Jefferson) Clinton (1946-   )

Bill Clinton became president in 1993. He had been the governor of Arkansas. Clinton promised to create more high-paying jobs for American workers.

HOW ABOUT YOU?

How would you like to be president of the United States?

Were you born a citizen of the United States?

Have you lived in the United States for at least fourteen years?

Are you at least thirty-five years old?

Those are the only rules for being president. So

The Marine Band plays at the inauguration of the president of the United States. The chief justice of the United States gives each president the oath of office in a public ceremony.

maybe you will be—
someday. All you have to
do is get elected. And
remember—being president
is an important job!

WORDS YOU SHOULD KNOW

ambassador(am •BASS •ah •dor) — an official representative of one country's government to another country's government

amend(ah •MEND) — to change by adding, deleting, or correcting

cabinet(KAB •ih •net) — a president's group of helpers, each of whom is the head of a department of government

conservation(kon •sir •VAY •shun) — protecting natural resources from incorrect use or destruction

convention(kun •VEN •shun) — a meeting of a group of persons for one purpose, such as naming a political candidate

dishonest(diss •ON •ist) — not honest; not worthy of being trusted or believed

elect(ih •LEKT) — to select, by voting, someone for an office or position in govenment

executive(ex •ECK •yoo •tiv) — the branch of a nation's government that sees that laws are carried out, appoints officials, and in general represents the nation to the rest of the world

illegal(ih •LEE •gil) — not legal; against the law

impeach(im •PEECH) — to charge a public official with illegal activities in order to remove the official from office

inaugurate(in •AW •gyur •ate) — to officially bring someone into an office, usually with some type of ceremony or celebration

judicial(joo •DISH •il) — the branch of a government that acts as a court to decide if laws have been obeyed or broken and if laws are right or wrong

legislative(lej •iss •LAY •tiv) — the branch of a government that makes laws

pension(PEN •shun) — regular payments of money to a person who has retired from a job

political party(poh • LIT • ih • kil PAR • tee) — a group of persons with similar beliefs who are organized to elect members of their group to office

politician(pol • ih • TISH • in) — a person whose profession is running the affairs of a political party or conducting the business of a government

politics(POL • ih • tix) — the actions of people who are primarily interested in electing representatives to political office or in controlling a government

resign(re • ZINE) — to give up or leave an office or job before a term is over

scandal(SKAN • dil) — actions that are offensive to the public

term(TIRM) — a specific length of time, such as that served by someone elected to office

trust(TRUHST) — belief or confidence in someone or something

INDEX

About the Author

Carol Greene has written over 25 books for children, plus stories, poems, songs, and filmstrips. She has also worked as a children's editor and a teacher of writing for children. She received a B.A. in English Literature from Park College, Parkville, Missouri, and an M.A. in Musicology from Indiana University. Ms. Greene lives in St. Louis, Missouri. When she isn't writing, she likes to read, travel, sing, do volunteer work for her church—and write some more. Her The Super Snoops and the Missing Sleepers *has also been published by Childrens Press.*